Contents

Introduction ⸻ 2

The Weather Bomb ⸻ 4

Juan's Ill Wind ⸻ 36

Springtime Was A Washout ⸻ 72

Published by Transcontinental Media Inc.
Editor: Kevin McIntosh
Art Director: Ted Lapierre
Digital Prepress Services: Toronto Shared Production Centre
Distributed by: Tall Ships Art Productions Ltd., Waverley, Nova Scotia
Printer: Transcontinental Interglobe, Beauceville East, Quebec
ISBN: 0-9736425-0-5
Copyright © 2004, Transcontinental Media Inc.
Printed in Canada

Cover photo by Paul Darrow
Photo Credits: Kevin Adshade, Mike Carson, John Christianson, William Clarke, Tina Comeau, Paul Darrow, Mike Dembeck, Scott Dunlop, Dave Glenen, Janet Kimber, Lana MacEachern, Jason Malloy, Brian McInnis, Vaughan Merchant, Sueann Musick, Darrell Oake, Andy Pederson, Kirk Starratt, Harry Sullivan, Heather Taweel, Wayne Thibodeau, Nancy Willis

D1069652

A year for the history books

Was it something we said?

Atlantic Canada is world famous for many things – magnificent scenery; warm and friendly people; outstanding seafood. Justifiably, it is also known for its unpredictable and often extreme weather.

As freaky as the weather can be, the region has never recorded a year of unrelenting assaults like it did in the 12 months from March 2003 through February 2004. Not one, not two but three vicious storms battered the area in that period. As people recovered from one blow another one nailed them on the chin. Any of those weather events, all on its own, would have made it a year to remember. Combine all three and you have the stuff of legends.

Springtime brought the floods, the worst in more than 60 years in some areas of Nova Scotia.

Six months later, closing off summer and ushering in fall, came Juan, the strongest hurricane to hit the region in 40 years and the most destructive ever.

Winter, brutally cold but otherwise uneventful to that point, brought the mother of all nor'easters, the most severe blizzard ever recorded in Nova Scotia and Prince Edward Island.

Floodwaters inundated Nova Scotia when as much as 124 mm of rain fell in one 24-hour period on to waterways and soil already saturated by heavy snowmelt. Homes and businesses were ruined. Roads and bridges were washed away. Lives were lost.

Hurricane Juan's visit was the shortest of the three but also the most violent. In barely four hours it laid waste to a wide strip through the most heavily-populated areas of central Nova Scotia and eastern Prince Edward Island. Boats of all sizes were tossed around like toys. Again, homes and businesses were destroyed. Forests, centuries in the making, were wiped out in minutes. Hundreds of thousands of people were without electricity for days. More lives were lost.

Weather forecasters issued dire warnings of a severe blizzard approaching the Maritimes. They only knew the half of it. In only 24 hours nearly one metre of snow was dumped on parts of the region. Gale force winds whipped the snow into drifts you could ski down. Nova Scotia and Prince Edward Island were encased in a brilliant white cocoon, effectively cut off from the rest of the wor

In the telling of these stories the supply of superlatives is soon exhausted. Things were the wettest, the deepest, the strongest, the highest. . . the worst.

Superlatives also apply to the people of the region. They were sim the best, weathering the storms then getting on with putting the world back together.

After a year like that Maritimers can be excused for keeping one e on the heavens as they go about their daily lives.

The year of the storms is now legendary. The trouble with most legends is that they are usually based on myth. This one is based solid fact.

The stories and images in this book are taken from the pages of Transcontinental Media's newspapers in Halifax, Charlottetown, Cape Breton, Truro, New Glasgow, Yarmouth, Annapolis Royal, Kentville. Teams of dedicated writers, photographers and editors put the legend on the record.

The Weather Bomb

It was a 24-hour stretch unlike any other in the recorded history of Nova Scotia and Prince Edward Island.

In the previous 12 months Nova Scotia had been swamped by the worst flooding in decades and both provinces had been badly rocked by a howling hurricane. As devastating as those events were they could only disrupt life, not stop it.

Then came the blizzard, the freeze-frame that stopped the action and wrapped the Maritimes in a smothering white blanket. Meteorologists call it a "weather bomb."

The snow started lightly overnight on February 18-19, 2004. It was a classic nor'easter the likes of which had not been seen in these parts. It raged across Nova Scotia and into Prince Edward Island. By the time it stopped, on the morning of February 20, it had rewritten record books and secured its place in history.

It dumped 95.5 cm of snow on Halifax, burying the previous record of 73.2 cm set in 1960 and the most since record keeping began in 1871. Charlottetown received 74.4 cm of snow, 20 cm more than the previous record set in 1973.

At the height of the storm wind gusts reached 124 km-h in Halifax and 104 km-h in Charlottetown. Tides along the Northumberland Strait and Bay of Fundy rose to 1.5 metres higher than normal. Both provinces declared states of emergency, a first for Nova Scotia.

Statistics Canada said the blizzard cost Nova Scotia employees 2.5 million hours of work. PEI lost 346,000 hours of work. Counting only hourly-paid workers, the economy lost more than $10 million in wages, according to the Atlantic Provinces Economic Council.

The Confederation Bridge linking New Brunswick and PEI was closed, a rare occurrence for the 13-km span.

Airports in Charlottetown and Halifax were closed. At one point there were 400 tractor-trailers lined up at the New Brunswick-Nova Scotia border because the Trans-Canada Highway was closed.

There were at least two instances when women in labour — one in Springfield, N.S. and one in Cole Harbour, N.S. — had to be transported from their homes in the buckets of front-end loaders to waiting ambulances. Snowplows led many other expectant mothers to hospitals.

A woman had to flee her burning house in Brackley Beach, P.E.I., as the blizzard raged outside. She was unable to call for help because her phone was dead. It would not have mattered because her road was impassable.

Awakened by the smell of smoke and unable to fight the blaze she threw on boots, grabbed a coat — but not gloves — and fled into the storm. She eventually reached a house half a kilometre away, her hands freezing, crawling on top of snow that was at times waist

high. She survived unharmed, but her house burned to the groun[d]

More than 30 people in Lower Sackville, N.S., shovelled their stree[t] by hand so an ailing 13-year-old boy could be taken to hospital if necessary.

Many people were stranded at home but many more were strande[d] at work. Hospital and emergency workers put in endless hours. Public works employees, especially snowplow drivers, were the ironmen and women of the storm.

Darren VanKampen of Charlottetown, only 15, thought he might d[ie]. A snowmobile trip with a buddy had gone bad, their machines stu[ck] in a drift and the friend gone for help. Darren got worried about hi[s] friend and struck off to find him. Hours later, hopelessly lost and exhausted, he took shelter under a tree. He was soon asleep and buried in snow.

Some time later he awoke and saw the lights of a search tractor. Unable to walk he crawled across the snow to his rescuers. Darren survived nine hours lost in the blizzard, relatively unharmed but with an experience that "definitely changed (his) view of how shor[t] life can actually be."

Canadian Idol auditions went on as scheduled in Halifax just days after the blizzard, when the city was still digging out and many roads remained clogged with snow. The show, after all, must go o[n]

With a newborn son in intensive care at a local hospital and two more young toddlers looking down from a hotel room window, Mark Johnston of Wolfville, N.S., found himself marooned in a Halifax parking lot. Help from Halifax Daily News staffers and several other good Samaritans soon had Johnston on his way.

Apocalypse now

Like a scene from an end-of-the-world science fiction movie, a lone pedestrian trudges down the middle of Barrington Street in the heart of downtown Halifax. The storm dumped 95.5 cm of snow on the city, making scenes like this commonplace for the few who could get out to see them.

Somewhere under all that snow is a car belonging to this Charlottetown couple who needed only muscle and determination to find it.

The scene — not to mention the aching backs — was the same in Halifax and on virtually every street in Nova Scotia and Prince Edward Island as people dug out from under the worst blizzard ever recorded in the region.

The museum ship Acadia weathered the storm at its berth on the Halifax waterfront.

Grounded

Transportation all across the region shut down during and for some time after the blizzard. Planes, like this one at Halifax International Airport, were grounded for two days because runway snowplow crews there and at Charlottetown Airport could not keep up with the relentless snowfall.

Where are we going to put all the snow, municipalities asked themselves as they began the massive cleanup chore. After receiving special permission from the Canadian government – for environmental reasons – crews dumped tons of snow into Halifax Harbour.

Like a ghostly apparition, a plow works a road near New Glasgow, N.S.

A machine in Prince Edward Island plows into the world of white.

Even the snowplows, like this one near Truro, N.S., sometimes met their match.

That's not a door this pooch is barking at,
it's a snowdrift at this home in Souris, P.E.I.

A blizzard is just a good excuse for this young seal pup to check out the Halifax waterfront.

Heavy machinery, like this backhoe in Charlottetown, was dwarfed by the massive snowdrifts.

Believe it or not, this is usually a busy thoroughfare in downtown Halifax.

Often, the best way to keep an eye on the cleanup efforts was from inside, through a window like this one in New Glasgow.

Prince Edward Island, like the entire Maritimes, became a world of ghostly white images.

Let 'er blow

The brilliantly clear weather that followed the blizzard made for some
spectacular scenes, like this one on Prince Edward Island.

The first order of business for anyone venturing out into the storm was to get a tight grip on your hat as gale-force winds whipped the snow.

Step lively
Snowshoes became the hottest trend in footwear.

It helped to have a bright paint job when you went looking for your car.

The phrase "winter's icy grip" was never more appropriate than at this location in Halifax.

Sometimes the knight who saves the day is not wearing shining armour and riding a glorious white stallion. Sometimes he's a guy like Chris McKenzie, dressed in a parka and driving a yellow front-end loader. When Melanie Edwards went into labour two days after the blizzard, her husband Taylor called 911 emergency dispatch. Their street in Cole Harbour, N.S., had not been plowed and there was no way any conventional vehicle was going to get in or out. They were told to prepare for a home birth. Despite the terrible conditions an ambulance, an RCMP cruiser and a snowplow arrived at the end of their street. McKenzie, the plow driver, carved a path along the treacherous street to the Edwards' front door. With the help of a Mountie and two paramedics Melanie was helped to the waiting plow and eased on to a bed in the bucket made with parkas, including McKenzie's. After a slow, cautious drive down the street Melanie was helped out of the bucket, into the ambulance and rushed to hospital. Seven minutes after arriving at the hospital Rachel Marie Edwards was born, weighing in at a healthy eight pounds, six ounces. Chris McKenzie was happy the delivery went well, but insisted he was just doing his job.

The tops of snowplows, just visible over the peaks of towering snowdrifts, were common sights for days after the storm.

The storm blew through, the sun came out and Halifax Harbour was a sparkling blue jewel — but even busy thoroughfares like this one were locked up tight for days.

Traditional Marine Outfitters in Annapolis Royal, N.S., was definitely not open for business in the wake of the blizzard.

When you have to push your snowmobile out of a drift you know the weather conditions are exceptionally bad.

Something as simple as a walk downtown became a harrowing ordeal.

With the schools closed there was time to deal with important matters, like determining who is King or Queen of the snow castle.

Peering out from under his many layers of protection, this youngster casts a long shadow across his frozen world.

Juan's ill wind

It was not supposed to happen that way.

The journey was supposed to weaken him, as it usually did to the others. He would weaken even more after arriving.

It would be rough because he would not go down without a fight. There would be things knocked over and water splashed all over everything. It would be the final desperate flailing of a dying bully.

That's how it was supposed to happen. Hurricane Juan did not play by the rules, ending up as the strongest hurricane in 40 years and the most destructive ever.

With occasional exceptions a hurricane blows itself out along the eastern United States. Hurricanes feed on heat, sustaining themselves on warm southern waters and the Gulf Stream. They usually become weaker tropical storms when they hit the colder waters of Atlantic Canada.

A meteorologist at the Canadian Hurricane Centre in Dartmouth, N.S., forecast that Juan would arrive as the weakest form of hurricane, with sustained winds of about 80 km-h and gusts possibly up to 140 km-h. It would quickly weaken into a tropical storm, he said. His advice was to close windows but don't bother boarding them up and definitely put away the lawn furniture.

This time, though, Juan found new life in a North Atlantic three to four degrees warmer than normal. That is all it took to turn a tiring storm into a raging, broad-shouldered Category 2 hurricane.

Juan's highest sustained winds, recorded on McNabs Island in Halifax Harbour, reached 186 km-h.

Juan made landfall in Nova Scotia at about 11 p.m., September 28, 2003. Within minutes it was roaring down the throat of Halifax Harbour.

It's arrival coincided perfectly with high tide, guaranteeing that its storm surge – nearly 3 metres in Halifax Harbour – would cause the most damage possible. A weather buoy at the mouth of the harbour recorded waves up to 19.9 metres.

It hit Prince Edward Island shortly after 3 a.m., still packing winds up to 146 km-h.

Juan hit the most densely populated areas of the two provinces – Halifax, Truro, New Glasgow and Charlottetown.

Two people were killed, one a paramedic in his ambulance, when trees crashed on to their vehicles. Five other deaths were later linked indirectly to the hurricane.

More than 300,000 customers of Nova Scotia Power Inc. were without electricity, some for more than 10 days.

Juan forced more than 600 surgeries to be postponed at the QEII Health Science Centre's VG site in Halifax.

Winds up to 138 km-h did not damage the Confederation Bridge linking PEI and New Brunswick. The 13-km bridge was closed to high-sided trucks but remained open to passenger vehicles.

Damage in Nova Scotia was estimated at more than $100 million and at nearly $10 million in Prince Edward Island.

The storm proved that nothing gets between Islanders and their politics. A provincial election on September 29, the day of the hurricane, had a remarkable 83 per cent voter turnout.

In Halifax 57,000 of the 80,000 trees in Point Pleasant Park were knocked down, leaving a scene of utter devastation.

A 158-year-old lighthouse in PEI, directly in Juan's path, was not damaged but had the paint stripped off its walls.

Diehard gamblers played on at Casino Nova Scotia, stopping only when the casino closed its doors the next morning.

The good new is there will never be another Hurricane Juan in Atlantic Canada. The name was dropped from the rotation out of respect for its victims and survivors. The bad news is hurricane season comes around every year.

The Larinda, a replica of a 1767 Boston Schooner, sank at its mooring in Halifax Harbour during the hurricane. The salvage operation was complicated by the fact that it sat on the bottom of the harbour for three weeks, near a sewage outfall that turned it into an environmental nightmare. It was refloated and is going through a long, slow, expensive reconditioning project.

Point Pleasant Park at the mouth of Halifax Harbour bore the full force of Juan's onslaught, losing 57,000 of its 80,000 trees. The scene of devastation was repeated throughout central Nova Scotia and eastern Prince Edward Island.

A precursor to Juan's arrival — huge waves crashing on to Nova Scotia beaches like this one at Lawrencetown — proved irresistible to this kayaker and others drawn to the power of the ocean.

A meteorologist at the Canadian Hurricane Centre in Dartmouth, N.S., tracks Juan's progress as it heads toward the Maritimes. The hurricane unexpectedly gained, rather than lost, strength as it neared Nova Scotia.

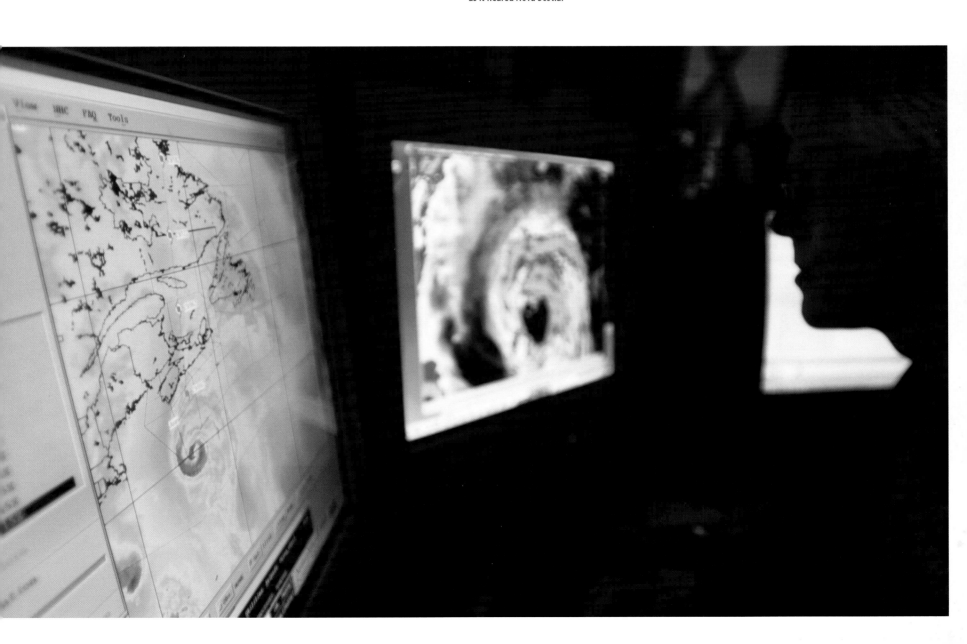

Wind surfing took on new meaning for these young people on the Halifax waterfront as Juan neared the city.

Barrington Street in downtown Halifax became a giant wind tunnel during the early minutes of Juan's race through the city.

Train traffic was brought to a halt by damaged railbeds like this on the Dartmouth waterfront.

With many rail cars damaged and even knocked off their tracks, train traffic came to a standstill in some areas.

Residential streets were turned into tangled jungles within minutes of Juan's arrival, leaving monumental cleanup projects.

Neighbours gathered, stood in awe of the damage, gave thanks for surviving the devastation, then began the task of reclaiming their streeets.

A man is surrounded and dwarfed by the remains of one of the oldest trees in Halifax, in front of the heritage property of former prime minister and Father of Confederation Sir Charles Tupper on Tupper Grove.

Cleanup workers, like this one in Charlottetown, had all they could handle turning big logs into smaller logs.

There really is a house under this fallen tree in Truro, N.S.

The $2-million replica ship Hector, defenceless in the face of the hurricane, was ripped from its mooring in Pictou Marina and driven on to the rocks. Hector, a replica of the ship that brought Scottish settlers to Nova Scotia in the early 1770s, sustained only scratches and a small leak.

This fishing boat at Pictou did not fare as well as Hector, ending up on the bottom of the harbour.

An uprooted tree lies amidst broken headstones in the Old Burying Ground, the first cemetery in Halifax, which dates from 1749.

Juan showed no more respect for the departed in Charlottetown, where a headstone lies smashed against the rocks.

An elderly Charlottetown woman peers through her front door at the mess that is her yard.

There was little many people – like this woman in New Glasgow – could do except survey the damage and wait for help.

Charlottetown Yacht Club was awash in floating and sunken debris. Some owners boarded their boats, hoping to ride out the storm and keep them as safe as possible during the hurricane. Others tried to tend to the boats but had to back off in fear for their lives.

Crews from HMCS St. John's and Army engineers pitched in to help restore some order to Halifax neighbourhoods. The hand-written sign on the car asks that the log not be removed from atop the car until it is seen by an insurance adjuster.

Halifax Parks Department worker Helen MacLean is dwarfed by fallen trees.

This scene is in Truro but it could have been any of thousands of streets across central Nova Scotia and eastern Prince Edward Island.

Hurricane Juan had a curious eye for architecture and landscaping effects as he roared through the region.

Even in the midst of the devastation and wreckage there were scenes of remarkable symmetry such as the snapped-off tree in Halifax's Point Pleasant Park and this toppled road-side sign in Bedford.

The military provided great help to public works crews and local residents in their massive cleanup efforts.

Light poles snapped like twigs during the hurricane, sending high-voltage electrical equipment crashing to the ground.

Pedestrians go about their business in Halifax, seemingly oblivious to the huge uprooted tree blocking the sidewalk.

Shipyard Road on Bedford Basin was hit hard by the hurricane as waterfront structures were turned into kindling in moments.

Like beached whales, large pleasure craft were strewn about lawns along the Northwest Arm in Halifax.

Boat owners at Charlottetown Yacht Club were left wondering where to begin in their salavage efforts as many boats were smashed and sunk at their moorings.

Springtime was a washout

Water will find its own level.

That's as true for an ice cube tray as it is for the Atlantic Ocean. It is true of rivers, creeks, streams and the ground under our feet. Water will find a place to go.

This was never illustrated more clearly than on March 31, 2003 in Nova Scotia.

Inevitably, 100 mm or more of rain in 24 hours is going to cause a lot of trouble. For reference, if you're standing in 100 mm of water your shoes are submerged and your ankles are wet.

Dump that much water that quickly on to waterways and ground already swollen and saturated from heavy snowmelt and you have the makings of a full-fledged natural disaster.

How bad was the flooding?

Two people were killed when their car was swept into the LaHave River in southwestern Nova Scotia. Three others narrowly escaped with their lives when their car was swept into the same river.

Salmon Hole, NS, recorded 124 mm of rain in 24 hours, the most anywhere in the region. The Salmon River crested at almost two metres above its normal level.

More than 200 roads in Nova Scotia were damaged or closed at various times. Forty-seven bridges were destroyed or damaged. Pictou County had so many washed-out roads they ran out of warning signs.

Because of the flooding, firefighters could only stand and watch as a business burned to the ground near Marshall's Corner near Truro.

The Sackville River experienced record water levels, one metre higher than those recorded in earlier floods.

A train line between New Glasgow and Cape Breton had to be closed because sections of the rail bed were severely eroded.

About 200 families in Quinan, a village in southwestern Nova Scotia were linked to the outside world only by boat for several days when a bridge over the Tusket River was washed out.

Scores of homes, businesses, schools, seniors residences and trailer parks had to be evacuated because of rising waters.

In the Upper Stewiacke area of Colchester County only one main road was passable "with caution."

It was the worst flooding in the area in more than 60 years.

Damage to provincial roads exceeded $10 million

Damage to personal property exceeded $6 million.

As always, Nova Scotians took the devastation in stride. It wasn't the first flood and it would surely not be the last. They very quickly got on with the task of putting their lives back in order. That's what people do around these parts.

Traffic — of all descriptions — was swamped by the torrential downpour.

Game called on account of boat traffic in the infield.

Even driveways were turned into surging torrents.

Many businesses, like this one in Bedford, N.S., became virtual islands during and after the storm.

If it floated it became a useful tool as workers checked for flood damage and began their repair work.

No mere pothole, the bottom literally fell out of this section of Highway 374 near Lorne in northern Nova Scotia.

Only the guardrails were left suspended across this chasm flushed from beneath Highway 374, one of more than 200 roads in Nova Scotia damaged or closed by flooding.

Firefighters tried to hitch a ride on a local farmer's tractor but in the end could only stand and watch helplessly as this North River, N.S., business burned to the ground. A half-kilometre of 1.5-metre deep water separated fire crews from the blaze.

Fire department rescue units used inflatables to evacuate residents from the rising waters of Nova Scotia's Debert River.

This motorist's short drive from Bible Hill to Truro, N.S. became more challenging — not to mention wetter — than usual.

This bridge near Upper Stewiacke was one of 47 in Nova Scotia damaged or destroyed by raging floodwaters, causing detours that lasted for months.

Only the ducks could get anywhere near the pedestrian bridge in this park in Sydney, N.S.

The highway through Hall's Harbour in Kings County, N.S., was turned into a very pecarious bridge over troubled waters.

Relentless floodwaters eventually got the best of this section of Highway 101 near Lequille, N.S.

The only good news for Carl White of Halifax is that he managed to buy the last sump pump in the store.

A blown-out windsock at an airfield in Shearwater, N.S., stands in silent testimony to the battering inflicted upon the weather-weary Maritimes during the 12 months from March 2003 to February 2004.